I0192773

Stop! You May Not Want to Open This Book

Comedic Evaluation of Your Habits, Time, and Money.

M M Rogers

Stop! **You May Not Want to Open This Book: Comedic Evaluation of Your Habits, Time, and Money.**

© **Copyright 2021 - All rights reserved.**
By M M Rogers

The content contained within this book may not be reproduced, duplicated or transmitted without direct written permission from the author or the publisher.

Under no circumstances will any blame or legal responsibility be held against the publisher, or author, for any damages, reparation, or monetary loss due to the information contained within this book, either directly or indirectly.

Legal Notice:

This book is copyright protected. It is only for personal use. You cannot amend, distribute, sell, use, quote or paraphrase any part, or the content within this book, without the consent of the author or publisher.

Disclaimer Notice:

Please note the information contained within this document is for educational and entertainment purposes only and may contain mature language and information. All effort has been executed to present accurate, up to date, reliable, complete information. No warranties of any kind are declared or implied. Readers acknowledge that the author is not engaged in rendering legal, financial, medical, or professional advice. The content within this book has been derived from various sources. Please consult a licensed professional before attempting any techniques outlined in this book.

By reading this document, the reader agrees that under no circumstances is the author responsible for any losses, direct or indirect, that are incurred as a result of the use of the information contained within this document, including, but not limited to, errors, omissions, or inaccuracies.

ISBN 978-1-7376687-3-2 Paperback
ISBN 978-1-7376687-2-5 Electronic Book Text | eBook

Midwest 2 U LLC
Matteson, IL – USA
info@midwest2u.com
www.midwest2u.com

Midwest 2 U

Table of Contents

Introduction

Honestly!

Given the title of the book, did you really think it
was going to be an introduction?

Side Note: This is short book. It's meant to be comical and
entertaining and provide you with a little bit of guidance. Thus,
you read on and try to understand what lies beneath the farce.

Chapter 1:

Really!

"There's never enough time to do all the nothing you want."   — **Bill Watterson**

Really!

You read through the introduction and continued to turn another page or listen.

Why?

Were you expecting this the book cast spell and make all your dreams come true?

Did you think you were going to open this book, find a $100 bill? You thought you'd experience such euphoria that you would scream out: "WOW! This is my lucky day."

Nope. This is your WOW moment!

This is a **thoughtless** phrase on a **simple** page with a **subtle** image above of what I am scornfully thinking. But you should keep reading.

You dare to walk in the face of danger. A thrill seeker.

You like to walk against the grain and into the forest at night without a flashlight.

I would say, you have a hard head. Maybe you are a bit stubborn more than most. You definitely don't like to listen or follow the signs.

What where you expecting? To find the keys to the city or to your future success.

Here is that key to your future success!

This is **another thoughtless** phrase on a **simple** page with a **subtle** image above of what I am scornfully thinking. But you should keep reading.

Or, maybe you are a treasure hunter and opening this book would give you a road map that will lead you to that treasure that will alter your life?

Below is the treasure you were searching for!

This is **another** thoughtless phrase on a **simple** page with a **subtle** image above of what I am scornfully thinking. But you should keep reading.

Hmmm.

Maybe you think you are intuitive or that your common sense and street smarts will guide you out of destitution into wealth?

It May!

But, let me ask you this?

Are you still searching for your abundance in an abyss of apps, video links, posts and podcasts, webinars and webcasts?

Are you making a comprehensive plan?

Keeping looking into the wondrous world nullity without a bottom in sight.

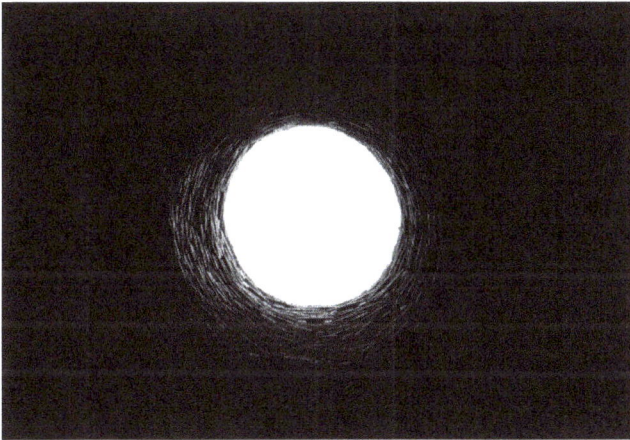

This is **another thoughtless** phrase on **simple** a page with a **subtle** image above of what I am scornfully thinking. But you should keep reading.

Like a hollow hole, an unproductive barren mind yields vacate habits, wishes and dreams.

How long did you stare into that abysmal hole searching a the hidden sense of hope and camouflaged secrets to your golden egg?

Here are your golden eggs!

This is **another thoughtless** phrase on a **simple** page with a **subtle** image above of what I am **scornfully** thinking. But you should continue on the next chapter

Chapter 2:

So, You're in Your Feelings Now?
But I Told You!

"We are slow to believe that which if believed would hurt our feelings."

- Louis Nizer

Are you hopeless in your feelings about this book?

Why?

You bought it...

And,

You opened it ...

And,

You are still scrutinizing the phrases on these sheets of paper.

This is **another thoughtless** phrase on a **simple** page with a **subtle** image above of what I am thinking. But you should keep reading.

Are you feeling baffled, dazed or upset?

Do you need to be muffed and knocked out of that virtual cloud you feel like you are in?

Don't be mean, and give it a bad review.

This is **another thoughtless** phrase on a **simple** page with a **subtle** image above of what I am thinking. But you should keep reading

FOR REAL!

But

I

Told

You!

Yet, still dumbfounded and moreover, you don't
get the hint? I literally cannot with you!

Worse off, you do get the concept and don't want to acknowledge the underlying principles in this book.

If so then **blah, blah, blah** and this is another thoughtless **phrase** and a **simple page** but you should keep reading.

I am laughing very hard as I lovingly say, "Child
Please. I told you. STOP! You may not want to
open this book."

You don't deserve **another** thoughtless phrase
on this page with an **image** of what I am
thinking.

I am not heartless.

I am sending you a little love while you attempt to formalize the theories behind this book.

Also, I applaud your will and need to fight to the finish.

It shall not be in vain.

This is **my heart** on a **simple** a page with a
subtle image above of what I am thinking

Chapter 3:

My Humble Advice

"I ordered a wake-up call the other day. The phone rang and a woman's voice said, "What the hell are you doing with your life?"

- Demetri Martin

Wake Up!
Wake Up!
Wake Up!

Changing our lives takes commitment and a healthy respect for tomorrow. It might seem like it's overwhelming or impossible, but it's not. It starts with creating some good habits. Once you have the habits down pat, you can start focusing on how you are spending your time. After that, it's all about your money.

As cliche as it sounds, there is no better time to get started than right now. The longer you put it off, the harder it's going to get.

Habits are ingrained over time. Bad habits that have been around for years could take months to get rid of. The longer you allow those habits to continue, the more difficult it will be to rewire your brain to get rid of them.

You're the only one who can truly make your life better, so get started on it. Stop watching television. Close down your email, games, Facebook®, Instagram®, and Twitter® accounts.

For once in your life, make bettering yourself and personal development the main priority. Especially if someone gifted you this book. It was definitely a hint to get your act together and start prioritizing for your future. All of this is in you, and you have the power to make changes in yourself. Nobody is going to do it for you.

Your Habits

Developing Healthy Behaviors and Inspirational Habits

When thinking about your daily habits, it helps to consider the things that you want to cultivate. If you hate starting your day feeling rushed and frazzled, set your alarm clock a half an hour to an hour earlier. This will give you plenty of time to get more accomplished, even if it's just a bit of time to sit and drink your coffee.

You'll also find the habit of getting to bed and waking up at the same time to be beneficial. Once your circadian clock gets on board with your new routine, you'll be amazed at what you can get accomplished in a day. So, take the time now to SET YOUR ALARM CLOCK.

This is getting mentally prepped for readiness every day. You'll be grateful for this later in life.

If you have a hard time getting things done, then make a daily, weekly, or monthly checklist. There are many apps out there that can help you with things like daily cleaning in your home. You can try *Spotless* or *Tody* to help get those regular habits under control.

Perhaps you may need to focus on your habit of negative self-talk. Nobody wants a Negative Nancy or Nate running their mouth in their mind.

This is something that could seriously hold you back from achieving your goals.

There are resources to help you to replace that negative self-talk with a more positive voice.

Cognitive Therapy, also known as Cognitive Behavioral Therapy in some cases, can be a powerful tool to use in your efforts to change the way you talk to yourself. It's never too late to develop a more positive inner voice. Tell Nancy or Nate to take a hike!

Some of the most successful people also practice visualization daily to help them get where they want to go in life. Oprah Winfrey uses vision boards to bring her goals to life. A young Arnold Schwarzenegger used to close his eyes and visualize himself with a rockin' bod.

It can work hand in hand with your positive self-talk. Once you start visualizing how you want your life to be, you'll find that you will start taking actions to make your life fit into what you are seeing.

So, take a look at the habits that you have and want to keep. Visualize yourself successfully practicing those habits day in and day out. In no time you'll turn your world upside down and you'll struggle to recognize the person you used to be.

Habits are so ingrained in us that they are subconscious. Grinding your teeth when stressed? Bad habit. Chewing your fingernails when you're anxious? Another bad habit. Reaching for the potato chips instead of the carrots? Yeah, I think you see where I'm going here.

It's easy to blame your circumstances on others, but put some onus on yourself. Get rid of the chips, keep your nails cut short, and figure out what's stressing you out!

You've got this. You just have to take it one step at a time.

Your habits drive your behaviors
and fuel your passions.

Exam your habit and behaviors.
They ultimately guide to all
your hopes, dreams, wishes.

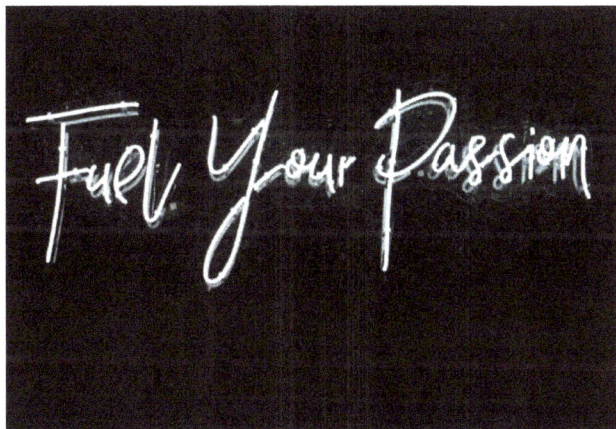

Your Time

Get the Most in Life with Productive Life Management

Speaking of time, are you wondering where it's all going? Scrolling through Facebook® or binging YouTube® videos for four hours might actually feel like five minutes, but it's not.

When you take a good look at how your time is being spent, you can find areas of improvement really quickly.

There is time for the things that are important to you, it's just a matter of fitting it in.

One thing people tend to blow off is exercise. "Who has time to exercise 30 minutes every day?" is a common question.

Well, if we're being honest, almost everyone can find another thirty minutes in their day if they choose to look for it and it will have benefit to them. See the above example of Facebook® if you're really questioning this.

Instead of hitting the snooze button three times in the morning, get right out of bed and go exercise. If you have your clothes laid out the night before then you don't even have to put any thought into it. Just get moving!

If you're stuck working in an office all day, try out a standing desk. Some companies might not provide them, but you can make it work with a shelf or a box. Already you've improved your activity for the day.

Want to spend more time with your kids? Well, then you might have to do stuff they enjoy doing. Minecraft might seem terrible, but if it's the thing they love doing then you should put some interest into it.

Some parents will join their children in the daily chores to spend more quality time with them. Want to hear how Robert's day went? Get him to help you make supper or take 10 minute to help him to wash the dishes.

Proper time management includes multitasking. Reading is an important hobby for many people, but let's be honest, it can eat up a lot of time. Grab an audiobook. Downloading it as an audiobook and turn it on while you're cleaning, cooking, or even while you're exercising. It also great background noise or motivation while a project that you keep putting off.

When you do things that way, you are managing your time to ensure you can accomplish the things that need to be done as well as the stuff you want to get done.

Time management is as much about thinking outside of the box and planning. It is being aware of how you want to spend your time and also the tasks require focus and complete that goal. It's about limiting any distractions.

There are some easy apps that you can use to help begin the process of time management. *Toggl* will time you on your phone and then sync up to your computer if you need it to.

You can also take advantage of some of the built-in programs on your phone. Most phones have a setting which you can limit the amount of time you spend on certain apps. Limit the time on the most distracting apps and you'll find an abundance of more time.

Nowadays, you can also take a look at the amount of time you spend in each app. Your phone holds a record for you, allowing you to self-regulate without hassle.

But be warned: It can be shaming to see how much time you spend on social media or playing games on your phone.

There's no need to reinvent the wheel, just use your new good habits to make the time in your life for the things that are important. You've got this!

**You time is OH SO precious.
Use it judiciously.**

Your time should be guarded and cherished,
after Faith and Family.

Don't let your time *go to waste*.

Your time is not garbage that you can recycle
for another day.

Your Money

Spend Your Money Expecting a Beneficial Interest and Return

Take a hard look at what you're doing here. The changes you make in this area will provide a quantifiable way to measure the quality of your life. There's got to be some dream of retirement in the future. or perhaps you want to experience the world. Your goal might be as humble as making sure your kids get through college.

In all of those cases, it starts with your own money management and the habits you have in place for yourself.

The easiest thing to do is start by making a budget. It doesn't have to be as big and complicated as it sounds. You don't need to break down every single penny that you're spending.

If you're looking at your bank account and saying to yourself, *"Okay, I need to save $400 for the car payment this week"* then you are already budgeting. If you're constantly asking yourself this question monthly, your budget is busted.

You can easily take it one step further and plan out all of the payments you have each month and make sure they are all budgeted for. Whatever leftover money you have can be used for the things you want to do.

But don't forget to save. Put some money aside for a rainy day (a little bit of fun). You never know when you're going to need some emergency funds. If you're going to play the credit card game, which many do with a lot of success, you'll have to be on top of your budgeting.

Paying for everything with your credit card can result in lots of free money and points. However, you have to make sure that you are still living within your means. Paying for everything with your credit card does not mean that you should be maxing it out every month. The goal is to successfully pay it off every month without incurring any interest charges.

You'd also do well to bite the bullet and go talk to a financial expert. They can help you make your retirement successful by giving you the guidance to know where to invest.

Investing is something that scares many people. The idea of risking your money in a market can feel a lot like gambling. But if you're talking to people in the industry, then you'll find that there is far less risk involved (unless you want there to be).

But let's be honest here. The true savings begin when you start making the small changes in your life.

Instead of eating out for the third time this week, why not head over to the grocery store and pick up two $5 pizzas to put in the oven? Everyone is busy and there are going to be evenings where you don't have enough time to make supper. Having leftovers in the fridge means you only need two minutes to reheat before you dig in.

If you're a smoker or drinker, you need to take a serious look at kicking the habit. Not only is it bad for your overall health, but it's hitting you hard in the wallet. Smoking two packs a day can be upward of $1,000 per month. That's a car payment. Or a mortgage. Or your share on an all-inclusion Caribbean trip.

Which would you rather have?

Another trick that many people overlook is spending more on quality items. For example, rather than spending $20 on a cheap pair of shoes you'll need to replace in a month, spend $100 on good quality. Those shoes that will last you a year or more.

Sometimes we get in the habit of thinking we're saving money by purchasing the cheapest items we can get our hands on. The reality is, though, you get what you pay for.

There's a difference between being frugal and cheap. One person is wise with their money, the other just doesn't want to part with their money.

It's time for you to take a good look at your finances and act like the grown up we both know that you are. Making a difference in your finances is as simple as choosing not to get the steak and lobster at the next restaurant and instead going for the humble burger.

It's as simple as choosing to stay in and watch a movie more often than going out and spending hundreds at theaters. Sometimes, it's as simple as shopping around for prices and ensuring you are getting the best quality for your dollar as you can.

Other times it will mean doing the brave thing and asking for a raise or trying to go for that promotion.

You get it. It's simple stuff and every change matters.

Don't squander or misuse your money.

Use your income with ambition!

Chapter 4:

Conclusion

"Knowing that one is always capable of change, the second step lies in making the decision to change. Change does not occur by merely willing it any more than behavior changes simply through insight."

- Leo Buscaglia

Ultimately, your curiosity and passion led you here. It led to you buy this book hoping for a nugget, gem or a guide to lead into the right direction.

Now that you've opened this book and read through it, you really **have no excuses left.** You know what you need to do and even know how to do it. Don't wait to start on this tomorrow. Procrastination is one of those nasty habits you need to kick. Get started now.

Make lists or a vision board, detail your goals, check your bank account often, and download a timer for your phone. See how long it actually takes you to start checking those off and adding new goals and vision. It's likely not nearly as much time as you believe.

Once you get on top of doing those things daily, you will have begun to ingrain the habits you truly need. Your mental preparation and personal development are the keys to your growth.

Come on! It's time to take those steps and make those changes in your life. There won't be any better time. And, let's be honest, you owe it to yourself.

What have your impulses done for you lately? Silly cat, why are you still reading or listening?

"To Live Will Be an Awfully Big Adventure."   *-Peter Pan*

About the Author

M M Rogers is incredibly passionate about enjoying the experience the world has to offer. After she suffered from a debilitating illness at the age of 29, she took a new outlook on life. She started placing added value in enjoying life, fostering and seizing her goals. After learning how to walk, speak and read again, she began to prioritizing more time into her personal development. Some of these successes has come from helping friends and family find their deep satisfaction in their careers, travel, cultural understanding, and LIVES!

She is a native of Chicago and still resides in Chicagoland with her husband and their American Staffordshire dog. She travels and writes under various pen names.

If you enjoyed this book, log into **midwest2u.com** and check out more up-and-coming authors ***and see free resources***.

References

Buscaglia, LF. (1972). "Love", Fawcett. Behavior Change Quotes. A-Z Quotes. https://www.azquotes.com/quotes/topics/be havior-change.html

Louis, N. (n.d.). Hurt Feeling Quotes. Wise.Sayings.www.wisesayings.com/hurt-feelings-quotes/#32234

Marks, J. W. (2021, June 3). Definition of Cognitive therapy. MedicineNet. https://www.medicinenet.com/cognitive_the rapy/definition.htm#:~:text=Cognitive%20th erapy%3A%20A%20relatively%20short

TOP 25 WAKE UP CALL QUOTES (of 63). (n.d.). A-Z Quotes. https://www.azquotes.com/quote/561641?ref =wake-up-call

Walden, L. (2020, April 26). 7 cleaning apps to help you organise your home like a pro. House Beautiful. https://www.housebeautiful.com/uk/lifestyle /cleaning/a32266236/cleaning-app/

Williams, A. (2015, July 8). 8 Successful People Who Use The Power Of Visualization. Mindbodygreen. https://www.mindbodygreen.com/0-20630/8-successful-people-who-use-the-power-of-visualization.html

Quotes On Wasting time. (n.d.). Goodreads.
https://www.goodreads.com/quotes/tag
wasting-time

Image Citations

Chaurasia, C. (2019). A heart (love) shaped carving on the trunk of a tree. In *Unsplash.* https://unsplash.com/photos/_PBW5ZyPiOA

Cohen, J. (2019). Boy In a Gray Hoodie. In *Unsplash.* https://unsplash.com/photos/_PBW5ZyPiOA

Du Preez, P. (2017). Black Pug Puppy on Brown Wooden Chair. In *Unsplash.* https://unsplash.com/photos/dOnEFhQ7ojs

Dziedzic, M. (2019). An old brass key dropped in the woods. In *Unsplash.* https://unsplash.com/photos/1bjsASjhfkE

Hill, V. (2018). Fuel Your Passion Text. In *Unsplash.* https://unsplash.com/photos/Z1HXJQ2aWI A

Lacoste, V. (2018). Hole In *Unsplash.* https://unsplash.com/photos/jNSJE8dMroo

Longmire, M. (2019). Spilled Coins from a Jar. In *Unsplash.* https://unsplash.com/photos/lhltMGdohc8

Valery, JP. (2019). Time lapse photography of several US dollar banknotes. In *Unsplash.* ttps://unsplash.com/photos/blOLCO2K4Mo

Villasmil, L. (2020). Young man covered in sticky notes, work overload. In *Unsplash.* https://unsplash.com/photos/mlVbMbxfWI4

White, B. (2017). Boy Wearing Gray Vest in Dress Pink Shirt Holding Book. In *Unsplash*. https://unsplash.com/s/photos/wow

White, B. (2017). Person Holding Blue Sand. In *Unsplash*. https://unsplash.com/photos/xqjMjaGGhmw

Book Cover Art

Book Cover Art. Clocks. (n.d.). Free stock images provided by Canva at Canva.com.

www.ingramcontent.com/pod-product-compliance
Lightning Source LLC
Chambersburg PA
CBHW071103040426
42443CB00013B/3379